the winnow magazine
Pittsburgh, Pennsylvania
www.thewinnowmagazine.com

Dual-Themed Issue: Home/Liminal Spaces

© 2022, the winnow magazine, all rights reserved
Fonts Used: Playfair Display
Cover Photo: Ed Inal

the
winnow

issue 10 / november 2022

home / liminal spaces

Dear reader,

We've all heard that home is where the heart is—for better or for worse. But where is home, really?

This is a question I've been asking myself throughout 2022, as I've been primarily focused on preparing for the huge step that is preparing to move out of my parents' house. As I walked deeper into the belly of the beast that is the American housing market, I dreaded never being able to escape my roots; home became a liminal space I would drift in and out of. And then something peculiar happened.

Last summer, once I graduated with my BA in English - Creative Writing, I began regularly publishing my work online. I met a lot of awesome people in the literary community on Twitter and elsewhere, and am continuing to build strong connections I cherish wholeheartedly. Suddenly, I was—and still am—determined to find each of my poems a perfect home.

Of course, each poem itself was like another house in danger of falling or seething in the void forever; my ghosts set words on fire, devouring their surfaces like vines, cumulating a giant mass of wreckage to be sunk in a lake or tossed away by a storm.

Eventually I found *the winnow* on a submissions hunt, and though I never submitted to them personally, I knew I wanted to be involved.

Now, I'm here, writing my first editor's note for a *winnow* issue. I'm even more sentimental than I thought I would be, and I am finally starting to believe I'll be okay: that I've found a home for myself within the wonderful *winnow* staff, and everything else will find its place eventually. I hope you enjoy all of these works that have been housed with careful consideration and an abundance of love.

Sincerely,
arden will
(any pronouns)
@ardentlywritten

Editorial Team

Founder
Rachael Crosbie

Editor-in-Chiefs
arden will
Rachael Crosbie
Meghan Flood

Managing Editor
Beatrice Winifred Iker

Design Editor
nat raum

Poetry Editors
Rachael Crosbie
Katie Veitch
Kayla Renee

Poetry Readers
Elizabeth Lewis
Anna Arden Williams
Ren Koppel Torres
Nishtha
Shay X. Gee
Catie Wiley

Prose Editors
Junpei Tarashi
Meghan Flood

Prose Readers
Hudson Hess
Ashley Bao
Adrianna Jereb
Anna Lindwasser
Camille Lewis

Art Team
Kayla Kazarick
Rachael Crosbie

Social Media Team
Rachael Crosbie
Anna Arden Williams
Lujain Benatia
Jesse Smith
Emily Carlson

Table of Contents

SECTION 3:

"Bein Hashemashot" - Kit Lascher

"The Small Hours" - Jennifer Martelli

"Outside In" - Amie Pascal

"The Ladder" - Robin Kinzer

"The Journey" - Robin Kinzer

"Missed" - Ash Bainbridge

"that's so liminal" - Eleanor Ball

SECTION 4:

"2:55am" - Taylor Yingshi

"There, There, There" - Kate Suddes

"Somewhere Between Nigeria and America; Saturday Drive on California Highway 138" - Dilinna Ugochuckwu

"March in Querétaro" - Monica Colón

"Jaipur" - Sagaree Jain

"Delhi" - Sagaree Jain

"Nightmares, Part III" - Sagaree Jain

"Epistle of Eve" - Arah Ko

"Yemma" - Nathan Pettigrew

SECTION 5:

"Peril" - Denis Harnedy

"A Football Stadium at the End of the World" - Lane Chasek

"In the Last Days of the Kingdom" - Maria Bolaños

"invocation of the mother" - Rachel Randolph

"Brief Encounters at 4am" - Dominic Hemy

"Afternoon Lull" - Ruthenium

"the past is a jean jacket" - Cloud Delfina

Content Warnings

"Ashtray" - domestic violence

"Sanctuary; revelations; If I am the flood," - body dysmorphia/gender dysphoria, police sirens, implied violence

"What happens to our photo albums when we're dead?" - OCD

"Dream House" - childhood trauma

"While the House Fills with Gas" - sex

"you may find yourself" - chronic pain, allusion to drowning

"rot around the edges" - implied abuse, dissociation, self-harm

"on differences in gay bodies" - violence, gore, hate speech, sexual content

"everyone has a queer farm fantasy" - brief mentions of animal death, fascist ideologies, smoking, trauma

"Lizard Man's Ranch" - Brief references to disordered eating, self-harm, and death

"Bein Hashemashot" - light mentions of maladaptive behaviors/coping mechanisms, such as substances, self harm, food issues, and suicidal ideation, themes of homophobia/transphobia

"The Small Hours" - death

"The Ladder; The Journey" - severe/potentially fatal illness

"Missed" - bereavement care

"March in Querétaro" - implied mentions of homophobia and mental illness

"Jaipur; Dehli; Nightmares, Part III" - self-harm, mental illness

"Epistle of Eve" - animal violence, miscarriage

"Peril" - references to violence

"In the Last Days of the Kingdom" - COVID-19

"Brief Encounters at 4am" - homelessness, swearing

SECTION 1

We Filled our House with pretty things so no one would notice the cold

Nostalgia

Suzanne Lavallee

Orange like a creamsicle, the sky melts. You sit beneath it, watching the sun vanish beneath a cover of fluffy clouds, swallowed whole like a dragonfly in the neighboring swamps. It's hot, you're sweating, and you can hear the crickets humming across the street. You know they're somewhere in the woods, behind the trees too tall to venture near.

They seem like foreboding mountains, and when you peer out your bedroom window you can imagine shapes like Maleficent. As the sun sets deeper and lower, they take on a whole new shape. That of a gaping giant with scraggly long arms. But you're not afraid because you know this street, and in fact this street is all you've ever known.

This street, the playground that heats up and seems to burn, the road to your grandmother's house (your best friend lives at the bottom of her street) and perhaps the highway that brings you to the extended family. But that highway is long, it seems to stretch forever which is why you don't drive down it very often, only twice a year. There are bridges that reach and lift you over the sea and billboards filled with colors like candy.

The sky purples, like a bruise on your knees and mosquito bites appear around your ankle. Maybe you shouldn't have worn flip flops. The driveway you sit on is still warm from the sun and you like to stretch the back of your calves against it.

You blink for a moment and don't think about how lucky you are to be here right now. The lights in the houses around you start to flick on and you can see inside to the neighbors kitchen. You've known them your whole life as well.

They're eating dinner and you think to yourself, I wonder what's to eat? The houses are evenly spaced apart, the road stretched for a while with houses that seem to mimic the other.

The sun has set and now it is dark. There's a fire somewhere down the street, someone must be making s'mores. Without a second thought you stand and brush the dirt from your leg, noticing a red ant crawled across your knee. There's chalk on your hands, it feels weird.

Like you rubbed your hands so hard the skin dried off and now there is only chalky bone. And it resides beneath your fingers like a cakey powder. So you walk into the house, aware that your knees now feel this way and there are little rocks embedded in your skin from the tarmac.

When you open the screen door, you realize you left your bike in the yard and you've always been told if you don't put it away someone will steal it. When you hop outside, the light above the garage flicks on, moths fluttering away. You don't want to keep feeling sticky with chalk so you drag the bike around back, where the woods tower over your head like skyscrapers or giants.

They are inhabited with many different things, coyotes and foxes... The bike can stay on the grass and when you're inside the house, you kick off your flip flops. The TV runs, but only static is trapped inside a box. There is macaroni and cheese waiting for you at the table, so you sit and eat it listening to the car headlights pass the house and the noises of rowdy teenagers.

There's nowhere you have to be tomorrow, or the day after that, or the day after that... So you take your time eating. You feel tired.

Sleepiness like a haze descends like a cloud over your head and right there reality starts to slip away. Something feels so unreal in this moment, it is as if you have been here before. With the sky dimming outside the glass doors and time so stretchy and perfect you could take a polaroid.

You take a bath instead of a shower and ever so slowly the perfect moment comes to an end like the chalk that washed away. You're going to grow up soon and when you do there won't be any way to get it back. The bubbles are frothy like the foam at the edge of a waterfall (much like the one you throw rocks into with your dad-He takes you for bike rides there) and they swirl up, nearly glimmering like glitter from a craft.

It's frightening and with ease you find yourself gripping the sides of the tub. The harder you hold the wet slippery tile, the harder it will be for this moment in time to pass, for it to become a memory. Gripping the edges, you look at your body and how tiny it seems, and think about your mind and how you will inexcusably be locked away from the way it perceives things.

The shampoo bottle is bright pink and has a princess on it, your nightgown lays across the counter, it is only one piece with little designs across it. Toys sit across the floor watching you bathe and for a moment you think how odd that is. That they are watching you. And watching you realize this wont be forever.

One more moment and you blink. And blink. And blink. And that night when you go to bed, there is the crushing sensation that when you wake up you will be an adult.

Of course, in the morning when you wake, you are not an adult. And everything you thought that previous night was just an idea much like a passing rainshower.

But one day you woke up and without even realizing it, you were an adult.

Ashtray
Max Gillette

My father owns a large glass ashtray.
It's green, except under August sun, where it smolders
like cobalt. Friday nights he tucks it against his chest
and totes it to our back patio to catch curled remnants
of cigars. Rest of the time it squats, vulturish,
amongst other junk—busted pens, unpaid bills,
lighters—scattered across the water-stained table.
Rare mornings I want to earn
gumball change, my parents pay me to dust
shelves, and I nudge the tray from its perch
to rest cool and solid in my hands.

Now, though, the ashtray twists towards
my mother's head. Suspended between the LEDs
and linoleum, it shimmers like a figure skater's skirt.
The green edge brushes her hair then crashes to the cabinets
behind her. Finally, it clatters to rest beside
the dishwasher. It's turned against us—offered up
its smooth, useless underbelly. In that distended mirror,
my parents' hands are raised. Their colliding reflections
tear across the ashtray's chipped glass.

my sister is a hoarder, but i love her
Madeline Langan

there's a dead woman's college diploma hanging in your bedroom that i had found, stale, marked with an orange sticker *$3.99* in a Katy, Texas Goodwill bin. when i found it, i told you that i was scared, that it felt haunted. but you didn't seem to think so – and if you did, you didn't care. i think if the phantom of a woman with a business administration degree from Auburn emerged from your wall, you would welcome her home. you let her in, after all. that's kind of how you are – you collect things, hold them. you keep dead lilacs, bottlecaps, words like *milkweed butterknife lamplit*, the quietness of a voice in hesitation, the tremble of a hand in shyness, stuffed underneath your pillow, your head, until they're warm, home. i think someone could live there forever, if they wanted to.

Sanctuary
Syd Shaw

I want to fill   my house   with blues
cobalt and pastel
shining on the tiles
I want to sit   to smell the kitchen air
I can feel my dreams   curdling
week-old milk on the table
swallowing all other scents

all my work   for two windows
 for unclogged drains and dishwashers
a painting   of forest creatures cavorting
before misshapen trees
in subdued shades
       my desires recede   like tides

I am not worrying   the floorboards
my fingernails are growing back
my family is three thousand miles away
enough   I tell myself
       to sleep safely

at night   when the could-have-beens claw
at the curtains I remember   my blue house
has two windows
no one has ever smashed them in

revelations
Syd Shaw

my heart is beating beneath the hum of the tv
and my thighs are always changing into
the wrong shapes. I split hairs
over how short I can shave my head
without looking like my father or
drawing his attention. as if that's the most important part.
my hands shake enough to drop mirrors and crack eggs
and I dislike the weak high sound of my voice. everything
these days is a symptom of something else, according to social media.

but have no fear; I like my clothes. enjoy dressing my paper doll body,
checking off the little box of beauty. detached, I scroll
the internet. I buy new pants, block old friends who post things
that remind me of chicago. *everyone should try HRT*, one writes,
just to know what it's like. that night I write a poem about eve
and the forbidden fruit. I cry into the shower drain, and the dirty water
carries my tears down the pipes, farther and farther away from my body.

If I am the flood,

Syd Shaw

you are the drought, the sun and earth
beating down on each other, laughing
at humans' cracked lips and raw throats. You
are the burnt-out hulk of a blind space probe
and I am the impact crater.

I am sitting down to a family dinner.
You are throwing up in toilets, fighting in bars,
pounding on car windows as I drive away.
You're a 10am cop call and a rotting pizza
in the fridge. I am the siren and the stench.

You are a heaping buffet plate, the glint of an owl's eye,
a woodchipper, trust fund, computer virus, black mold.
You expand with pride, become every highway
and landfill and landmine. You are everything
and I am the white spaces   between   surrender

What happens to our photo albums when we're dead?

Christopher Wellings

Elsewhere, trying to be clever, I called them plastic carousels
of former lives. But it's just the same lives at an earlier stage:
innocent faces and questionable fashions pressed behind
a chemical sheen. What happens to this photograph of us
with Gaynor – where the banks of the Ouse cradle the river,
its memory of silted lung. From that day we walked Virginia's
footsteps, and a swan descended from the low grey sky.
You were sure it would pull up and when it didn't we staggered,
laughing, from the path of its wrecking ball swing.
Now your lashes are jewelled with tears, and I realise I
have had a head start: it is not in your nature to expect disaster.
My audacious disorder thinks: *could I have saved her?*
Maybe if I'd kept this fear closer? Or arranged these pictures
in a luckier order? And finally my voice answers: no.

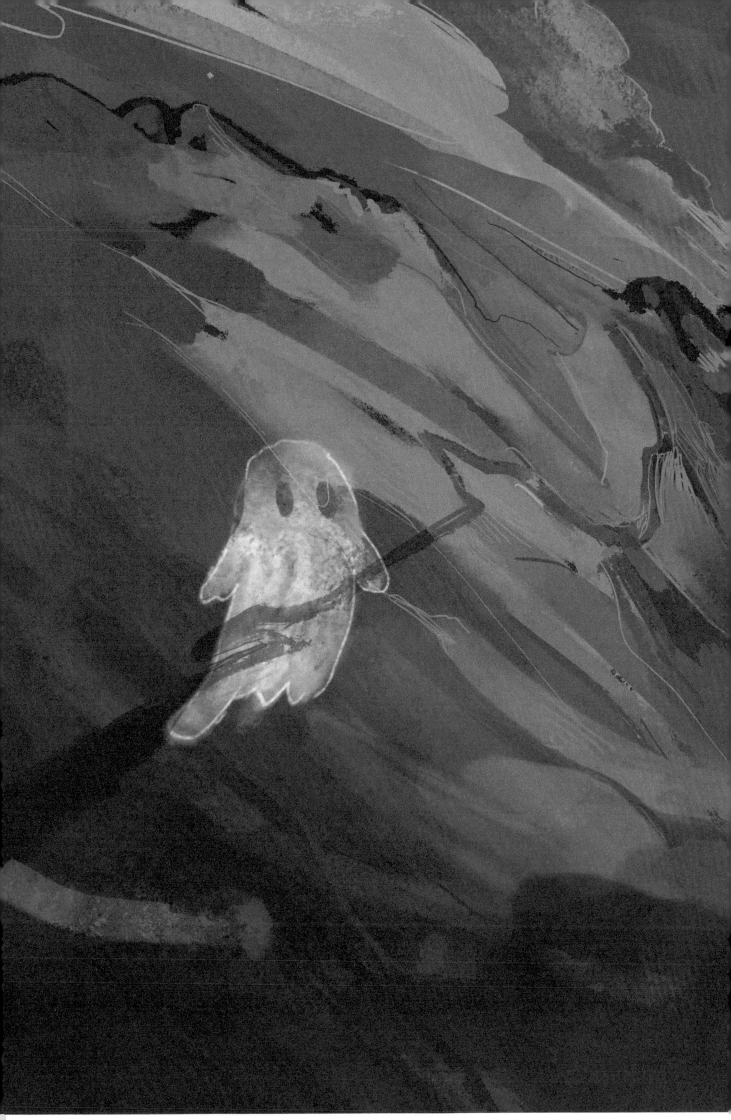

While the House Fills with Gas

Julian Guy

I roll my jeans down legs, you're still stuck
on the knots of your boots, and soon
the rented room looks lived in. Clothing
everywhere. You inside me. We suck hickies
onto chests. Make fists of blankets.
And when Mark knocks, saying the house is filling
with gas, we stumble untied into the street.
Laugh down to ocean water and palms
scraping a bruised sky warm. Sit on the edge
of plaza, between families roller skating,
teenagers kissing, women selling sandwiches
and cookies. Alfajores crumbling in my pocket.
God at our backs. There is not much else to say.
For a while, we were happy.

Run Home
Rachel Alarcio

My home of nearly two decades is going to be demolished tomorrow, and even with Extra-Strength Benadryl, I can't sleep. So I jumped the garage fence and jimmied the locks with my old keys. I'm in my old unit now, A17, and it looks exactly like it used to and completely different simultaneously. Of course, there's no furniture. Just the white kitchen island straight out of the eighties remains, which I'm perched atop as I type this on my phone. Somehow, the LED streetlights with their yellow tinge and low hum aren't isn't comforting white noise but B-roll for a B-list horror flick.

I feel like Schrödinger's cat, neither dead nor alive. Suspended on the invisible thread between dusk and dawn. In my mind, Mom's calling me a little crybaby after I punctured my foot on a spiky nail at age six. In my mind, I'm back when Dad was still alive-alive, not Schrödinger's-alive. Then, I open the bathroom. The nails embedded in the wall are still there, and there it is on the floor: a silver-gilded framed picture of Henrietta, Mom, Dad, and I with the glass screen shattered to bits. We didn't take this with us for a reason. Mom kept insisting we forgot it in the clutter.

I stare at Dad's gap-toothed grin and Henrietta's hand on my shoulder, then at the empty kitchen where we used to make blueberry and banana pancakes with honey as a late-night snack during the ungodly hours of Sunday morning. I hear a dog howl, maybe out of hunger, maybe out of loneliness. I say my goodbyes, to the house, to Dad, then shut the front door behind me. The walk to the back area of the property is a eulogy, with my phone flashlight the lone candle, the lone source of light in absence of the building lights. Then, I arrive. The (now dying) rose garden and empty pool with grout and dead branches and dead leaves greet me. I find a gap in the chain-link fence, slip through it, and run home.

I know everyone got lost in the mall once
Simone Parker

but I never did
I got lost in a big old house
where the people move like ghosts
and the stairs groan with vanished voices.
I slipped into the cracks between the floorboards
with the dust mites
and watched the enormity of shoes passing over.

I'm sure that someone came looking for me,
peeling back the plaster skin,
searching this wood skeleton for a trace.
I hate to say that it was too late

but the house held me home
and it's hard to wriggle out once you're in
(like when your head gets stuck in the banister
so it must fit
but somewhere between the wooden posts
it must have morphed).

I've changed,
grown into the wood grain
made my home in the asbestos
breathing in the things
you lost beneath the radiator.

I know everyone got lost at the mall once
and was found.
Through the warped windowpanes
I watched them come home.

you may find yourself

nat raum

i'm high and tired and the list of things i care about is dwindling by the minute. i will wake up tomorrow sore-hipped and wristbones wailing for giving in, but this sort of restless demands i abandon my prescribed posture pose and corkscrew my limbs until my body is a shorehouse to be swallowed by the sea. sometimes i will wake between now and then (sometimes more than one time) and my throat will lurch through the kind of cough where you spit mucus like slugs, chip itself dry until i reach for a flat nightstand seltzer. when the last of my pieces have finally drifted again, my synapses will remember that i absolutely cannot help myself from being crushed by the sorrow of stasis. i will turn over and instead of blinking away hours when the black of my vision splits into dots, i will face the flood that carried me here, no matter how high i've built my stilts or how many floors i've climbed. i will tread in riptides and remember i am not actually standing as still as i think i am. i'm just in the same place as always.

rot around the edges
nat raum

today i heard the corpus christi churchbells
in the county, christ's very own
bodybells chiming a solstice christmas
in my head. what i felt was kind of like

the way i cry whenever i read something
too pure on twitter because i just want my own
chance to be wholesome. the phantom chimes
are here to remind me i'm still corporeal

on this marble where the internet does not care
what you hold dear. it will break you if you let it
(just like he did). i only have feelings anymore
when i'm reattached to this body through some

sort of quiet anguish, like flaking skin from my
lips with flattened cuspids.

on differences in gay bodies
Camden Beal

you inhabit two personas

And I – remembering this hate you carried toward me crept deep into my organs

<damn, who let the faggot in the chat?> (1:00pm, 54s) heart

lungs and spleen,

– searched for the better half,

the delicate fawn newly birthed

or the crying hen plucking her own feathers, your face against the windowsill

made me realize I never had to show you my love.

Shimmering shadow of you.

I knew you hated me for a reason.

See trickle down economics.

See the HIV pandemic.

See how cigarettes are called fags

because they're something to be burned.

<I've been losing myself, nowadays. Trying.> (me) (1:00pm 56s)

see how gay bodies are not human bodies

because the qualifier always comes first,

because it separates the two

Separates my boyfriend and me as we walk down the street in crisp leather doc

martins and meditate on what it's like

when high schoolers just shy of adulthood

yell "cock sucking faggots"

and mutilate this sacred space between his hand and mine.

yet we are not the ice and salt you want us to be.

<i don't have a problem with gay people,
only when they're all in your face about it> (1:01pm, 37s)

in the morning when i sat with my boyfriend and he looked
at me
saying i love you
his left eye squinting
from the glint of sun scoring the window
my arm wrapped around his shoulder
like a snail
i noted that my love exists in a space of emptiness
a space of impermanence

of days spent laughing through meadows and
crawling through tunnels
our love is the kind of person who writes poems only in couplets.
You made these institutions to solidify the remains *<just don't touch me with the*
same finger
you stick up your boyfriend's ass> (1:02pm, 1s)
of the dead to put money through generations
and can one say our love exists
when you only want its
absolute dissolution?

society runs us through a filter, a colander,
like we were water
as though purifying us would bring us
to our most perfect form.

<as if I'd want to touch you at all> (1:02 pm, 3s)
but we resist this commodification.
we resist the decades of being called
gay best friends *<fag>* (1:02pm, 5s)
so that others
could find comfort in our existence.

we take our water bodies and slip
<it feels wrong to be anything, anyone but myself.> (me) (1:03pm 4s) through
the cracked stone
so one day we can break through these plexi-glass barriers. so that one day we
can erode them to sand,
melt them in their stance
<can we get an f in the chat?> (1:03pm, 7s)
<too late, I'm already here.> (me) (1:03pm, 17s)

Fraxinus
Ash/ley Frenkel

Growing up I worried
that my tits would never get so big
                              big enough
                                    enough for who I can not say

((Have you ever pulled your hair back and looked in the foggy post-shower mirror
thinking
                    Huh, I look like a boy))   whatever that means

I remember hearing, after the fact
a memory of a memory
that in my ultrasound my father could swear
I was a boy - I had his legs!
                              (turns out I don't)

All the old ladies from the neighborhood told
my mother the same because she was carrying
just so
and yet

When I came into this world I was marked my mother's daughter
and I am still my mother's daughter
but I am also so much more

Do not call me ma'am and do not call me man
if you must call me anything call me fraxinus
call me being of a thousand emanations call me love

Wrapped in rasped laughter knowing eyes careful mudras
my presence is an incantation that in its multiplicity
unfolds the seed of myself

A caterpillar in metamorphosis
fluid self-digestion on the soles of my hands and feet
and the things that I think I know are just things that other people think they know

And the person who I am is also the person who I am becoming
though not the person foretold
in the memories of my makers

I am a sculptor of my own design
and whether clay or wood or bone or feeling
I can spin the im/material into words that convey the myth of my origins
not a hero's journey but
a long and meandering walk along forked paths lined with towering milkweed

The cells of my flesh
flit into monarchdom
a pollinator's wet dream
and I am reminded   all things turn to ash
                              that with incineration comes possibility
          what a blessing it is to know uncertainty

everyone has a queer farm fantasy
Nico Wilkinson

until the sink is full of dishes
and the virus makes its way in
and the dog has shit on the floor
and a chicken is disemboweled again
and someone needs to peel her from the dirt
and someone needs to dig the hole
and someone needs to gather the bloody feathers
and

i am happy to be here most days.
like when we went to waffle house and
on the way, someone jumped out of the car
to scrape a nazi sticker from a street sign
before the light turned green
and we laughed despite the fact that this city
is full of nazis but
it's full of us too.

it's late spring and the goats are shedding and want
nothing more than to be brushed and chased
around the yard. i think of them
rolling their eyes, making sense
of our antics: the humans
need enrichment again.

there are extra hands to build the greenhouse
and pro-abortion campaign signs from november
to patch the roof.

the piano plays and fills the every room
with the sound of what lies beyond survival.

type-a gays beware: this house shakes and moves -
literally, one side is sinking - and we gotta move
with her. this old queer crone: risen in 1905, mother
of stucco, basement of brick and mouse skeletons, keeper
of us.

the sun hits her
and her doors once again fit in their frames
and she feels young again, even as we
step out of the shower, sweating. one day,
i tell her, i will buy you a brand new AC system.
but until then, we'll smoke on the porch
and we'll dance outside with the goats
and we'll step around each others egg shell edges
knowing each of our pet peeves comes from
one of our pet traumas, running amok,
their claws clicking against the hardwood.

Lizard-Man's Ranch

Colleen McDermott

The meadows bucked like mechanical bulls. Sloping up and down, golf-course-green, out of place in high desert. Arroyos coughed out arrowheads from their flaked layers, like the earth had no use for them anymore. Mountains dominated whatever was distant. Us? We got the trees. Russet ponderosas leapt upwards like skyscrapers, but our group of five, city-goers as we were, never made the comparison. There was no need to. Sometime during the first week, at the end of a long workday, I looked at the trees and those people and said, "Have you guys realized this is probably the best job we'll ever have?"

You may have been to Lizard-Man's Ranch. There's an even better chance you at least know someone who has. It's one of the largest youth camps in the world, attracting over 25,000 people to its trails each summer, and yet for those three months it felt like something I alone could keep. In base camp, a sign over the door at the registration headquarters spelled out the ranch's motto in daisy letters: CHANGE LIVES. I always liked how it never specified whose.

Limp hair, lidded eyes, pills, pills, pills. Two traumatic brain injuries and this ugly shopping list: icepick headaches, nausea, mitochondrial disorder, fatigue, poor vision, nutrient malabsorption. The day I left, she was scheduled for three surgeries the next month, to get the nerves in her head cauterized, burned off completely.

I didn't know if I'd like it at first. In fact, only two days into our week of conservation department training in the backcountry, I was ready to give in. The views were stunning, but the pure air still hurt, and the hike to our campsite alone had pilfered all strength from my calves. Nuggets of hail jabbered the ground without pause; our bosses woke us from our tents at four AM with screaming chainsaws, splitting our dreams in half. When I learned to operate one of those chainsaws myself and that one tree careened backwards, needles brushing my face as the death-trunk missed me by half a foot, I sat on a rock and cried and swore I would quit. Leave. Like I had anywhere better to go.

I think it was one of those evenings in the training week that kept me at the ranch, all seven of them spent huddling in soaked clothes and slurping dinner from collapsible silicone bowls. We shared stories and learned about each other, then. The Wisconsinite wouldn't shut up about his home state. Submarine Syd served in the Navy and spent six years in, well, a submarine. When he complained about his tent having flooded the night before, someone's raucous voice replied, "Ah, well, you're used to waking up underwater!"

I have symptoms of my own: a hatred for mirrors, an addiction to the things I hate. Has the roll of blubber on the right side of my back reduced any fraction overnight? Can I see my hipbones, at least? Pulling out from the skin like sprinters stretching their necks to cross over and break the victory ribbon first? This disorder's no race, but I would give anything for a finish line.

When participants come to the ranch, they spend over a week with their home crews trekking through its beautiful backcountry. Along the way are stops at primitive camps, to try their hand at a myriad of activities: horseback riding, black powder rifle shooting, homesteading, mountain biking. One day of that adventure must include a three-hour conservation project, for we believed having the right to enjoy land should include shouldering the responsibility to take care of it. That's what I got hired to do: educate dozens of kids a day on forestry and wildfire, then watch with measured concern as they wielded sharp saw blades in the field. Voila: "conservation."

We got split up after training, groups of five thrown together and stationed at different camps. Ours specialized in astronomy. We were driven there in two mud-flecked pickup trucks. That first night, before the stars would bullet-point the sky and distract us, our infant work team sat beside our canvas tents and introduced ourselves for real.

Joe of Time ended up at Lizard-Man's Ranch because he loved the outdoors. Everything about it—mountains, trees, animals, streams—except for the fact that once on a hike his best friend stepped too close to a precipice and fell hundreds of feet to her death.

Apple was there to further her career. She'd just graduated, after all, with degrees in environmental studies and ecology, evolutionary, and organismal biology. Plants didn't judge her, not like some family members back home.

The Blond didn't get to say much. A few words in—"Hi, I'm the Blond, I have ADHD, I get bullied a lot for it"—and he broke into tears, couldn't finish.

O Great Leader, our foreman, was the only one of us who'd worked at Lizard-Man's Ranch before. He had so many great memories from the previous summer. When he thought of them, he didn't feel like hurting himself anymore.

I went last. By then, the trend was obvious.

What else am I running from? A muddy bricked dorm building. And that window in my room, which heralded the sight of a thousand other college freshmen having no problem making new buddy ol' pals in "unprecedented times."

Cheeks streaked with grime, the same kind of high desert dust that could otherwise be shoveled into a vessel and displayed on a bookshelf, sold in a curio shop. Clothes roasting, strata of sweat and campfire smoke and piss and freeze-dried black beans rolling off the fabrics as they approached. Posture sagging beneath the weight of backpacks as well as the argument they'd had a few miles back. The crews of tweenagers weren't often in a tremendous mood when they arrived for their conservation project, which meant we had to serve as comedians as well. They usually hooted when we called Smokey Bear an eco-terrorist, so out of left field it was. They liked coming up with their own names, too, for the hand tools we presented. Once, when I held up the log tongs—a metal claw meant for lifting felled tree trunks—a young boy beamed and christened them "Dr. Big Fingers." I don't think I've scream-laughed like that since.

We worked for eleven days at a time, then made the most of three days off. Without cars, we had to rely on the wayward commissary truck or mail delivery to take us back to base camp, and for the most remote site on the whole ranch, that was always a gamble. Before our first "weekend" Joe of Time and I begged our camp director to try to coordinate a ride for us over the radio. It didn't work. What's more, a few days later the manager of the ranch sent a message to each of the backcountry sites forbidding that kind of "nonessential broadcast." Joe of Time and I bore it together, as we did all things that summer. We laughed with a goodhearted irritability, because nothing was ever truly wrong or bad out there. Not even a scaly manager with venom in his veins. Over dinner one night, he got a nickname too, just like the rest of us. "You win this time, Lizard-Man."

I call myself straight, but more and more that feels like the Catholicism of my upbringing talking. People have teased me for years over my lack of sexual awareness, and I'm sure I could figure it out if I tried, but it hurts just to think about.

For my 19th birthday, we set up blankets in the meadow and snagged all the tortilla chip bags we could find. There were no crews in camp that night—no kids to worry about, for once—and no clouds either. My astronomer friend Kansas Freddie Mercury (it didn't hit us until he grew the mustache...) showed me

Jupiter in their cavernous telescope, then Saturn, then a few pixelated galaxies. And I thought space was supposed to make you feel unimportant. Later, Apple made me a cake and gave me a pocket puzzle, wrapped in a Ziploc bag, and I saw the best shooting star of my life—long, blue-tailed.

The Blond liked to play guitar, but he only really knew one song. He sat in his tent with a canvas flap open to repeat those chords something like a million times, while we groaned and yelled at him to shut up, or at least learn something new. Apple called it our love language.

We had the weirdest conversations in those woods. After O Great Leader started playing history podcasts for us, we talked of Romans and Mongols and Germans, of empires fallen. Other times, it was plain nonsense. Once during a lunch break, with my butt against hard-pressed dirt, my back against surrendered bark, dipping veggies in a swath of peanut butter, Joe of Time told me, "You know, our fingers are as delicate as baby carrots. We could easily snap them in half, but our brains just won't let us."

"Eyes on the future!" "It'll get better!"—how, when it feels like I dropped something important a long time ago and never went back to pick it up?

Just a few days into the summer, our bosses, the Ninety-Sevens, had ventured up to our camp to check in on us. They'd ended up staying a while. It was like living with your high school principal or something, that need to treat every motion and word to a hyperbolized vigor. Joe of Time felt nauseous one of those days, and he didn't ask to go back to his tent until he'd thrown up for the seventh time. When the Ninety-Sevens made the same trip two months later, it was sure different. They caught us leaving the worksite a half-hour early. So be it, we were languid as the cattle, carefree as the clouds. United. At large. We owed no one the respect of authority—not our bosses, not the urban lives we had left behind.

Inside jokes were aplenty. Mostly we yelled at each other random funnies we'd overheard from the kids ("Your hairline is an OSHA violation!"), or favorite lines from the skit performances camps far south of us put on ("I'm a fishmonger. I mong fish. Every day I strap on my monging galoshes…"). Whenever she did something wrong, Apple unfailingly threw two fingers to her chin and asked, "Am I a clown?" Joe of Time and I particularly loved reminiscing on the last day of conservation training, when we outran a livid thunderstorm only to find out our bus wouldn't arrive to pick us up for another two hours. Lizard-Man himself rode up then in his own gleaming pickup truck and chuckled past a forked tongue, "Man, y'all are about to get dumped on!" before driving away.

There were other friends: Trail Jesus, Corn on Ja-Cob, Ohio. We saw them when we reassembled in base camp for our downtime, three days to go absolutely anywhere. Often it was across the nearby state border, for the dispensaries. Once we drove five hours across high country only to shop at a T.J. Maxx, get some ice cream, and sleep in a Quality Inn's last two rooms. Sometimes we just drifted right back into the wilderness; it had everything we needed.

And I never want to leave.

To imagine Lizard-Man's Ranch, you have to first imagine a terrible idea: take all these angsty young adults, toss them among the mountains with no supervision, and then entrust to them the safety of 25,000 children.

CHANGE LIVES. The kids' and our own.

For a few months there, I thought we'd really done it.

***

This is real life: touch the crown of my sister's head, and she won't feel a thing. The nerves were burned off, remember?

Things began shifting when I walked out my tent one morning and couldn't see the mountains through soupy grey. Thinking it was fog, I didn't pay it much mind at first. But the haze was still there by afternoon and evening. It covered our stars. Fog, I realized, is supposed to burn off. This stuff just burned.

The mirror in my new dorm room is even bigger than last year's. I try to eat healthy, but carrots don't remind me of fragile fingers anymore.

Every night, base camp relayed news over the radio. Harmless stuff: Shaquille O'Neal pays for a stranger's engagement ring! USA takes home the most gold from Tokyo! There was never anything about wildfires snarfing up the whole West.

Loneliness returned quick, my constant company. I think about the others and if it hurt for them too, transitioning back to the city like this, where our regular, boring names are expected yet never said enough.

The last few weeks of the summer, our talks to the kids took on a darker tone to match the sky. They didn't laugh as much. "For over a century, we suppressed fire. Now, that policy is coming back to bite us full-force. You see all this smoke? That's what's coming. Sometime soon—and we do mean soon—this ranch is going to burn to the ground."

I've come out as asexual and agender. A couple questions answered, even more opened up.

Liminal spaces aren't meant to last. Escape, ownership: all temporary.

I pin a map of the ranch to my wall, along with some pictures. For a time, this place existed, and I within it. That's all.

Be glad we got one summer away.

Bein Hashemashot

Kit Lascher

Talmudic Definitions of Twilight (Bein Hashemashot)

a) It is a period that is possibly day, possibly night. According to this definition, the concept of twilight is wholly a product of our ignorance of the precise point at which one day ends and the next begins. Nevertheless, our ignorance results in special laws that apply to this period.

b) It is an admixture of day and night: a time-period in which day and night overlap, so that it possesses both qualities.

c) It is neither day nor night, but an entity of its own, which effects the transition from day to night and from one day to the next.

- Lubavitcher Rebbe, Rabbi Menachem Mendel Schneerson; adapted by Yanki Tauber.

I am not trying to convert anyone to anything. There is no agenda. Jews don't convert. Inverts don't convert.

Inverts?

An inversion of proper gender roles. It's a word that has fallen out of use. I think if we can reclaim "queer" we can reclaim "inversion."

What are you inverting?

We are women who love women, so we are playing "men." We are men loving men, so we are playing "women." And we are. . . whatever I am. Playing at whatever I'm playing at.

So where all these inverts coming from?

Where do you think I came from?

 I know you. You're not like the others.

I felt that way too. And I didn't know where to go or how to express that. So I found people who loved me for my rigidity. Who welcomed me, encouraged me. We just love black and white. I don't care about the xeroxed copies of copies of worksheets that tell me black and white thinking is a cognitive distortion. Nothing I got in a manila folder in a hospital could ever understand me.

Why were you hospitalized?

Ha.

I'm serious.

I don't want to talk about that. I want to talk about the in-between.

In between hospitals?

Sure. I live in between hospitals. When you're there? You just get to a point where you can live. And between? You learn about dialectics.
A dialectic is two seemingly contrasting truths which are simultaneously true. Someone with my brain wants easy answers, extremity, right and wrong. If I can find a group that thinks exactly as I do and sees the world the same way I WON'T FEEL EMPTY ANYMORE.

I'm fine. You're the one who's sick.

Yeah. Okay. You're fine.

Everything I do is to fill a void. People. Drugs. Self-harm. Starvation. Suicide attempts. If I'm in pain at least I'm feeling something. I attract rescuers. I love having a favorite person. You're my everything. There is nothing worse than alone. You are my savior. I don't need a higher power. You're it.

Making a person your higher power is a terrible idea. And a way to avoid the in-between. The moment at the bus stop before a doctor's appointment. The breath of silence before clocking in for your shift. If I always have someone to talk to, I won't be alone with my thoughts. If you have thoughts like mine, you understand the value of this.

 I don't make other people my higher power.

How are you getting your opinions about a higher power?

Everyone I'm talking to is extremely knowledgeable.

You think I fell for my exes because of their lip shapes?

I'm not gay.

Understood. Do you want to talk about saints instead?

What about them?

When Joan of Arc said she was seeing and hearing angels who told her to lead armies, the people in charge had to assess whether she was a witch. If she was really hearing the voice of the devil.

They were able to assess that it was not the devil but they couldn't tell if it was really God. These people were, after all, human.

Once everything went awry, they gave her a choice. Repent, admit your heresy, never wear men's clothes again, and we won't burn you.

She tried. But ultimately her allegiance was to her angels and not to men.

When she put on men's clothes again, they said she had "relapsed." They had no choice but to kill her.

Now she is canonized. Her miracles are recognized. She is the patron saint of the country she sacrificed everything to liberate.

Are you comparing yourself to Joan of Arc?

Why not? I reject the idea of "relapse."

That's probably why you keep relapsing.

You do not go back to the way you were. You are not your behaviors. An alcoholic who has a sip of champagne does not "go back." If they don't stop there will be problems, of course. And they should work to reduce or eliminate a behavior that causes them and their loved ones problems.

It's fine if the idea of a relapse helps you. But, as you can see with Joan of Arc, it is up to humans to decide what a relapse is. And humans make mistakes. The people who tried her made a mistake. They have now changed their mind. Clearly. And if they had been able to move past extremes, you're either a witch or a saint, maybe she could have lived to see 20.

You're right. They were wrong. But they weren't God.

Neither are you.

. . . . . .

Maybe I am going to Hell.

I don't want that for you.

I have been a woman. I have been a man. I have been a creature. I have been everything to everyone and now? I reject all of it.

I have no identity. I love who I love and do what I do and try my best to help others. If identities help them, who am I to say they can't hold those? It is in no way my business.

I fight like hell for others. I Venmo people who need it. I speak up when a customer in my store is profiled. I collaborate with people who understand how it feels to be unseen. Unheard. Disrespected.

I am not for everyone. I do not have mainstream appeal. I will always be too much for some. And that's okay.

I know nothing. There are special rules for twilight because of our ignorance of it.

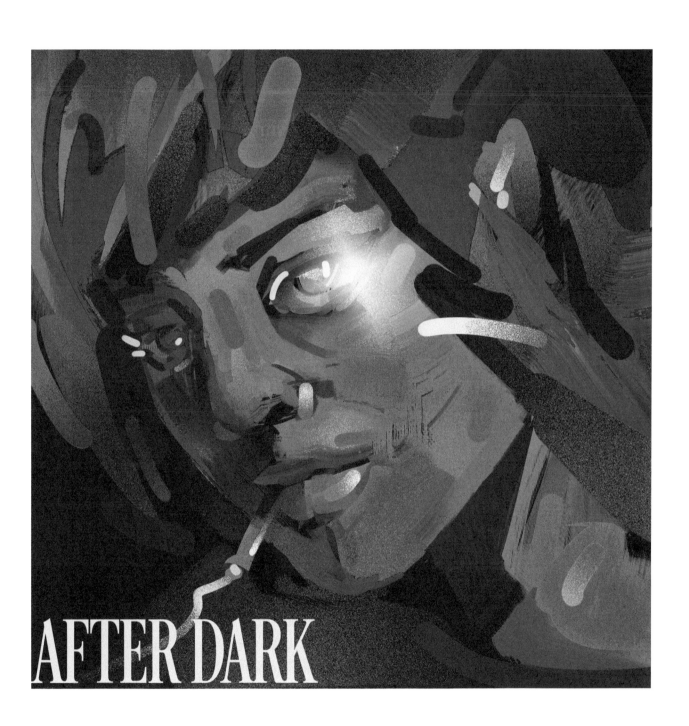

AFTER DARK

The Small Hours
Jennifer Martelli

A boy's ghost dragged himself from the harbor
side of the causeway. His body, broken and pronounced
dead hours before at the hospital, his car

hauled out of the water and towed before the sun
came up over the beach. The ghost, confused,
returned to his first house, the one he lived in

when his father held his bread-warm
bundled body above the lattice fence
to show me: *Look at my baby boy.* I swear,

I saw him while I was up, thinking of red silk thread
and conspiracies to connect. He hid
by the juniper bush near the fence by his old backyard.

There is a before and after for us, the living:
one day, one hour, one minute, the second
before it happens, and then the connection to after

floods like the causeway during those full moon
high tides and freak rains that shut down
passage. Perhaps it is different for the dead,

though who could bear those endless
small hours? I cried when I saw him trying
to get home, and for his mother, who is stranded

in the after, but more for me. In my second sleep
of the night, I tossed loose change to him and old
candies shaped like eggs, rabbits, maple leaves.

The Ladder
Robin Kinzer

(1.)

I was raised in a glass house in the woods. There from
birth— child of sun and ivy, spoiled by sunlight casting
hazy rainbows on warm wooden floors. The angled glass
houses, jeweled boxes, red maple leaves and fuchsia
azaleas echoing themselves over in every window.
Here, hickory trees even sprout from the middle
of our deck. My father hangs a basketball hoop
on that same grey stretch of deck. Brings me a plump
brown ball. He plays with me; teaching me to dribble,
to take a jump-shot, a three-point shot. A pretend,
giggling sort of hoop shot. We play at night, golden shadows
cast across our leaping forms, outdoor lights buzzing
like beetles above us. When I spring into the frosty air,
I imagine myself as Tinkerbelle. My father, Peter Pan.
Grinning in the lamplight, about to take on Captain Hook.

(2.)

The biggest tree on our land is a lumbering willow oak.
Years later, a massive limb of that tree will crash through
our house, and across all three cars, including the dusty
old Ford pickup truck I'd previously thought invincible.

(3.)

I'm seven years old. The willow oak stands tall,
tire swing loping from its largest arm. My father,
in the dark again because he works two jobs, pushes me.
Our laughter ricochets through October air.

(4.)

The arguments are the most surreal part about growing
up in a glass house in the woods. Other glass houses
cluster close, leaning into your windows. Sometimes,
I wonder if a furious version of my father and a wailing,
teenaged version of myself will forever live in those walls,
trapped in time. Moths in amber. Now we're flushed
with forgiveness, but I can still see us, screaming throats
hoarse over music too loud or dishes too long left undone.

(5.)

A few years ago, my father, in his late seventies,
built a mesh enclosure that slants, musical, around
the place where we used to dribble and dance.
Now, my parents eat summer breakfasts outdoors;
halved grapefruits, English muffins with marmalade.
Keeping just cool enough, metal fan chugging above.
He's re-built or remodeled some two-thirds of our
childhood home, lowering shower doors and bathroom
sinks as the years snuck by us all. They want to stay
in this honeysuckle-circled house, beloved by wildflowers
and fireflies alike. At eighty, chemotherapy pills spilling
through his veins, my father is finally slowing down.

(6.)

The other day, I saw him putting a cap on a thirty foot
tree they had to slice the rotting top from; the white oak
that's long knelt over my parent's dented silver mailbox.
Only this time, my father stayed on the ground, oversaw

my brother-in-law as he scrambled up the ladder
and around the tree. It was the first time I ever
saw my father take the easy job. The first time
I watched him hold a ladder with aging, spotted hands.
Where before, he always climbed and climbed.

The Journey
Robin Kinzer

We prepare for our trek: water bottle, mango smoothie,
car keys, a book for my mom to read in the waiting room.

It is a familiar journey. The pavement rivulets before us.
An occasional pothole. A deer, cumulus tail quivering
in the summer air, making a mad-eyed break for it.

I envy the deer, momentarily. I have forgotten how
to be daring. Illness slurped that marrow right out of me.

We arrive at the pain specialist's office. (Or is it
an oncologist, an infectious disease specialist, a psychiatrist?)

No. It is the pain specialist. Where we go the most, where
we accomplish the least— monthly visits firmly required.

In the doctor's office, a middle-aged woman bends and clunks
a plastic skeleton, tries to explain the mystery of my spinal pain.

She only briefly mentions endometriosis, abdominal agony
that tugs my uterus around an enraged, embittered clock.

(Several failed endometriosis surgeries under my belt,
it will be another decade before someone says: *You need
to get a hysterectomy. The pain won't stop until you do*.)

I take the frail blue pieces of prescription paper like onion
skin between my palms— oxycodone, fentanyl— these sad,
limp badges of a medical system that's given up on you.

My mother's smile, sweet as tea in the deepest South,
never fails to greet me after an appointment is over.
The shame, glue in my bones now: how often did I not smile back?

I don't notice the glimmering pink nubs budding from her
upper back until much later. Pain makes even magic hard to see.

Post-appointment duties are many and varied.
She has grasped my shaking shoulders as I cry, her frame
so slight that even my sick-body feels thick against hers.

She has rejoiced with me upon finding possible answers, laughing
as our voices ricochet joy around the innards of the station wagon.

Once, she even screamed at a doctor for me, rifling around
in the dusty root cellar where she keeps her rarely used yells.

But mostly, we listen to Joni Mitchell and Dar Williams,
while driving to the pharmacy. Maybe first, a fast food soda.

After Atlanta, after the hysterectomy, I see her midnight flight.
Watch her coast from oak to elm. Smiling, I keep her secret:

There, tucked a few inches beneath her shoulders, luminous nubs
that detonate into bloom. A glorious spray of gold feathers
that umbrella wide open— wider— propelling her to air.

Missed

Ash Bainbridge

A silver sequin
missed.
Just a scuffed dull glint,
tucked beneath the delivery bed
on hospital vinyl.

My fingers pinch,
already stiff from fridge-room temperatures and
cool raw-sausage leg
that gained no warmth from handling kept minimal
     or plaster hand and foot casting,
        or cellular hand-knitted blanket.
Cuddle frozen around
a paper kite
crafted –
     just for her –
        with learning hands at nursery.

His gift was sunshine yellow
with rainbow sparkles and raindrop glitters
now
     ablaze
        against each soft black fingernail.
To diamond base, a woolly tail was taped,
plaited like hair with the fortune to grow.
Messy play, so
his sibling could fly to heaven

in a plastic bag.

Nostrils prickle crystalline
with Clinelle
    and ice-blue Cuddle Cot tangs.

I cannot bin
a silver sequin
missed.
One of dozens
spread with gummy plastic trowel in mitten fist
and stuck with sticky toddler grief
    not yet felt and they'd no doubt inherit.

I cannot return or entrust
a silver sequin
missed.
She'd left –
    wheeled to rest
    in the hooded sable pram, snuffing out staff chatter.
Her spirit had left –
    via the window prized open to the safety-latch inch,
    as is tradition (and, I suspect, so no-one else follows).
Their midwife had left –
    burning out from guiding others drowning.
Her parents had left –
    alone
        to collect the kite's creator
        and try to explain why the second car seat was still empty.

that's so liminal

Eleanor Ball

after "Let's Play Superliminal | ContraPoints Live"

[my voice has been chosen specifically to remind you   i do not care.]

i watch you eat sushi. bite the salmon's pink flesh, slurp seaweed salad. delicately wipe your lips. on the back of my tongue, the ghost of a flavor i never liked.

that's so liminal.

piano music creeps in like overflowing bathwater / the kind of music that lulls you to sleep / the kind of sleep that gives you a headache / i got 8 hours the last 5 days and i've had a 3 day migraine / maybe the next room will cure me / aleve balances on my dry tongue, melts and

makes my mouth bitter

water soda / excedrin soda / heaven soda / hell on earth soda / supersocialist soda / superliminal soda / past & prologue soda / soda as dreams are made on / soda rounded with a
sleep

that's so liminal.

you watch me eat sushi. bite the salmon's pink flesh, slurp seaweed salad. delicately wipe my lips. on the back of your tongue, the ghost of a flavor you never liked.

hold / right / click / rotate / drop
breathe in   lean back   free fall
through the haze
touch me   touch you   your hands come away oil & blinding color   & that's so
liminal.

[just popping in to give a quick update on where you are. you still don't know.]

There, There, There

Kate Suddes

It started with a podcast. Although to say it started there is not exactly true. One headphone in her ear, brushing her teeth in someone else's bathroom. She rewinds; 15 seconds plus another 15 for good measure - makes sure she heard it right. The host cues up the artist with a question that could be answered in any number of ways. The artist takes a sharp inhale and begins:

Ugh, or maybe it's, *ahh*. Exhale. *I mean*. Pause. *I'm glad I haven't been put in that position*. And then she laughs. *I'm like, you know, I mean.* Pause. *There...there... there...* She says it three times...*are people that I love very deeply*. She did not say loved. *And because of how things ended, we don't*...pause...*speak anymore. And it breaks my heart to this day that that's just the way things are. Umm. So, I could not imagine shedding that much of myself, um, or*...pause...*being in a room with that person again in that way.*

But this is where she knows they differ. Because this is what she imagines all the time. For now, she spits out her toothpaste in a renovated sink. She wipes the counter with a stained washcloth and slides under someone else's sheets. She falls asleep and dreams of that lucky accident, the good fortune of finding herself in the same room. Dreams of dry knuckles pumping gas and then in her hair. Dreams of happenstance in a strange town, in an unfamiliar state. Dreams once of J. Lo and Ben walking toward her on a sidewalk. Jen leans in and whispers, *it can happen again*. A dream, she knows in her bones, of a day that will never come. But she keeps returning there anyway because it's the only place they have left.

Months go by and when she listens again, she notes the title of the episode: *Ode to Duets*.

Somewhere Between Nigeria and America; Saturday Drive on California Highway 138

Dilinna Ugochuckwu

There is fog everywhere. The sky is full of pearl-gray clouds.
The fog swallows mountains.

Mountains which are thoughtlessly beautiful. So green. The
world looks so green here —

I'm not used to this humidity, I'm not outside but just looking
through the car window,

I can feel water vapor on my skin. The world is moving on
without me. In the distance the street curves into

Lagos again. My mother agrees. A man walks, unafraid,
in the middle of the road,

with two daughters, holding baskets full of water bottles.
A car in front of us slows down, taking what they offer.

March in Querétaro

Monica Colón

Another day of straight white classes
in this straight white cohort. I walk home
under lenten jacarandas and think of
what I'm missing: blazing crabapples,
candling daffodils, fresh wet violets
in ditches. The house finches flew north
already, leaving me drowning in sun.
Among eggs and nopales, I think
of folding dumplings with friends. Between
classes and excursions, I tongue syllables from
my three English books—Emily, Kaveh,
Seamus—until understanding returns, palpable.
I dream of light on ice, boots on snowmelt,
scarves stuck in zippers, laughs pouring
out of the third-story window.
As I walk, my feet dodge bees. They've thronged
to the sidewalk for the cotton candy
of fallen blossoms. If there is a God, I
am asking her: preserve me from buzzing
at pavement when the jacarandas are laden
with purple. Teach me again to delight
in leaves and shadows. When I touch
my sternum, tell me I am still who I am.

Jaipur

Sagaree Jain

We all have our stories. And on the
side of my taciturn father—
lordship, courtship, kids shipped off
to the States. Jains preach

on non-violence and vote BJP.
My Dadi names herself three servants
and they all have second jobs.
I speak these truths not to

confess, not to absolve, but to note
that wealth is pulled from the earth
and its people. They pulled these forts
from the earth and its people

to do the violence they could not
protect us from. This pink city,
city of sordid jewels
and straight weddings. I walk out

into the heat and they name me
American, one by one, until I wear
my own skin draped around my
shoulders, hiding me from harm.

I return to someone's home
and see only the workers
sweeping the floor, eating alone.
My Dadi asked me what happened

to my forearm, how could I tell her
I paid for our sins? Not that I'm Christ
on the cross, staying in heritage
hotels, asking the teeming masses

to make me chai. I was born,
but I was ripped from my mother,
and from that I have never
recovered. Cities rise, and they are ripped

from their people, and for that
they make no apologies. Oh Jaipur,
city of my sins, city of my silly
penitence. From you, I learned to step

softly in the temples. From you,
I come, from you, I return.
From you, I bare and then cover
my aching breast.

Delhi

Sagaree Jain

After Arati Warrier

When I tell my people I'm going back,
I mean I'm tired of traveling up and down

the umbilical cord, not knowing where
my mother ends and I begin. When I tell myself

I'm going home—maybe that means Delhi, Dilli,
dilly-dallying about in the oppressive heat,

in my oppressive caste. When I tell my great aunts
I have no man, I learn to look into the void

and lift up my skirts, unzip my zips, dance lonely
and brilliant and bare. I was never meant to return

with such ferocity and insistence
to all these expired empires. I say

my prayers. I pay my penance. I see your twisting face
and raise you my twisted sorrow. In my ancestral home,

built of mirrors and mothers, I wait, doing my best
not to hide. Once, I tell them all, I was not shameful.

I was tender, I was glorious. I was stars constellating.
I was rivers meeting in the middle. Push, they told

my mother, and I was mortal once more.

Nightmares, Part III

Sagaree Jain

In my dreams, I am back where safety
became boredom, where white walls led
to white walls, where a woman

with trailing hair wailed, "I've been here
for six months." In my dreams,
there is no money reminding me of the price

of my difference, no dull revelation
that sin costs. In my dreams, my monsters take shape
and they all look like bills from the psych ward.

Can you afford to breakdown? I can
and always have. Wealth spilling green
at its edges, red at its core. Did you ever ask

not to exist? I did and always have,
salt seeping backwards into a warm placenta.
Do you ever wake to monsters? Face bare,

rib cage broken down the breastbone. In my nightmares,
once and just once, I was whole. I was heavenly.
I had no more or less than my loved ones,

I had a place to rest. And outside my window,
in the garden of Eden, my beloveds came and went
as they pleased.

Epistle of Eve
Arah Ko

I'm not sorry for the fruit.
Instead, forgive me for the rib
wasted on my muddied flesh.
I'll never know how much you bled
in that grassy sleep, or upon
waking, how loud your long
and wordless scream. Forgive
me for the snake who always seems
to follow in his twining way, scales
flecked with dusk, eyes so smooth
and lidless, I couldn't see
the lie. You know I'd accept sunk
teeth again and again to undo
that one. Sorry more, for the children
we buried together—twins devoured
in my womb, Abel engulfed
by his own wheaten field, daughters
scattered, like ashes, over many waters.
Sorry for the times our feet bled
on the dusty road, for the flaming sword
seared into every dream. I'm sorry
to have learned shame, and known
myself to be naked, heard
and lost the great voice in the garden,
watched our sons sink
past the sun-brushed horizon
until my eyes stung in the light of it.

But my love, I'm not sorry
for the fruit. Husband,
you ate it, too.

Yemma

Nathan Pettigrew

History says our civil war began in 1991, but my junior high school was set on fire in the spring of '89, and Yemma got us out of the country once riots and destruction became public executions.

Sad to leave Algeria, I believed Yemma's promise that happiness was waiting for us in America.

"It'll be good, Nuna You'll see. *Inshallah.*"

My birth name was Nassira, but in Yemma's eyes, I was always her Nuna. In terms of blood, she was my grandmother, as my parents had died in a car accident when I was a toddler.

I didn't remember much of my parents, yet my memories of the Mediterranean miles from our house in the suburb of Hussein Dey were crystal clear. We'd camp on Tipaza Beach, awoken by seagulls. My parents would hold my hands and swing me over the shells, the water so warm and split into two shades of blue, the brighter like sapphire surrounded by glass reflecting the sky.

Jamil lilghayih. That's how my parents would describe it.

Their place in Jannah, Yemma had explained, was guaranteed since they'd passed during Eid.

My earliest and fondest memories of Big Eid were of Yemma taking me to get our hair done. After the salon, she'd bring me to the souk and buy me a new dress with any pair of shoes that fit my big feet. I barely slept in those days.

Yemma had inherited her wealth, and she'd made investments, having moved me to her courtyard in the Casbah of Algiers. Yousef Lamri would prepare a feast while other neighbors sang the classics. I'd play darbuka with the children, the air bursting with turmeric, cumin, and cayenne and a pinch of *ras el hanout*. From tajines, we'd eat our lamb and couscous after saying *Bismillah*.

Enjoying baklava for dessert, we'd listen to Yemma tell stories about the Revolution.

Refusing to call the French our enemy, she would single out the reign of the Fourth Republic and their agenda to erase our religion, our history and identity while taxing us for our land.

But the notion of going to war for independence had divided us, and the land takers had used that advantage, turning our people against each other.

Bloodshed between our communities had claimed an entire decade before the fall of the Fourth Republic. Our women had put the pieces together, producing an infrastructure of safe transportation, food, and housing for anyone willing to join the Liberation. Our women participated in combat, showing our men the correct targets to focus on.

"Our women were heard around the world," Yemma would tell us. "We were the ones on the news chanting *Yu! Yu! Yu! Yu! Yu! Yu! Yu!*"

Women and children in the courtyard would repeat her chant. "*Yu!! Yu!! Yu!! Yu!! Yu!! Yu! Yu!!*"

To help me fall asleep, Yemma would burn bakhour and massage my curls with olive oil.

Jamal Zidane was the neighbor who collected rent for her. A Berber from the mountains of Tizi Ouzou who'd fought with Yemma against the land takers, he went missing after my school was set on fire and Youssef Lamri convinced the courtyard that Jamal was responsible.

Our independence in a growing number of eyes was nothing short of an illusion. Unless willing to learn another language, our people were prevented from securing high paying jobs.

Fed up, *hittistes* took over the streets, and violence became our new climate.

Youssef claimed that Jamal had tried to frame the *hittistes* for my school in a desperate attempt to divide "real Algerians."

"But I know this man," Yemma said publicly. "I know Jamal like I know my Nuna. No, Youssef Lamri is looking for a sacrifice."

Mobs and sacrifices, she explained in private, were nothing new, the misguided ones who'd reduced my school to ash no different from the ones who'd crucified our prophet Jesus.

"Muhammed—*sallallahu alayhi wa sallam*," she said, "asked that we sacrifice only the worst of ourselves while remaining thankful for Allah's blessings." "*Alhamdulillah*," I said, ashamed for failing to see my school burning down as a blessing.

Under a cruel and blinding sun, Youssef Lamri dragged a naked Jamal Zidane into the courtyard like an animal with his hands in rope.

Neighbors gathered without protest, without questions or a conversation. Men and children threw rocks and slashed Jamal's face and forehead.

I tried to look away, but Yemma pressed her fingers into my temples. "Eyes open, Nuna."

A terrifying moment, as Yemma had become a stranger and scared me the most until the execution ended in fire, Jamal screaming and screaming while the courtyard cheered.

My insides erupted for everyone to see, and Yemma carried me on her shoulder to our bathroom.

"You have nothing to be ashamed of," she said, cleaning me up. "That was my same reaction the first time."

She flew us to her brother's loft in Vincennes and waited until our second night in town to paint the full picture.

"We're never going back," she said.

"Even if things die down?" I asked. "Inshallah."

"*Inshallah*, Nuna, but that could take years, and I didn't win a war for you to fight another."

"So, we're living with Uncle Mustafah forever?"

"Only until I can get us to America," Yemma said. "*Inshallah*."

A promised land where differences were celebrated, and where all people could prosper.

That's what I'd learned about America before seeing my school **was** attacked.

On her knees, Yemma took my hand. "Do you see now? Why I made you watch? And why we can never go back?"

I burned the *bakhour* and allowed myself to enjoy the olive oil.

We landed at Logan International on my fourteenth birthday.

"*Mabruk*," I said, and Yemma laughed.

"*Mabruk*, Nuna."

She bought us a small house in Natick where we spent most nights enjoying *Indiana Jones*, *Aladdin*, and *Back to the Future*. I'd break down with Elliot when watching *E.T.* and reach for Yemma's hand. She took me to Fenway years before "Sweet Caroline" became the park's theme and made me pray a decade later for the clerks in Stop & Shop who'd harassed us for wearing hijabs after 9/11.

During Little Eid of 2019, Yemma went to sleep and didn't wake up, leaving me the house. I'd called her Yemma, but the birth name of the woman who'd done everything in her power to protect me was Rhanya.

She didn't live to see America so divided or a mob storming our Capitol or a pandemic reshaping the world, but Yemma did see English become my third language.

America seems on the verge of tearing herself apart, and maybe I should consider flying away, but this is the home Yemma gave me and the freedom she would've fought for if she had to.

I think of her hand taking mine on the flight to Boston.

"It'll be good, Nuna You'll see. *Inshallah*."

"*Inshallah*," I'd said.

"But we should also be thankful," Yemma had said, "for the blessing of our journey. *Alhamdulillah*."

Our journey at that point had brought us to a place where we could hold hands above clouds with the sun shining on our faces.

"*Alhamdulillah*."

Peril

Denis Harnedy

The moon is full
and I am floating
above a field
near my house.

There are wolves
but if I concentrate
I can remain
out of reach.

It is hard
to know how
to concentrate
properly.

Wolves know
the smell of fear,
the taste of blood,
the heart pounding.

A Football Stadium at the End of the World

Lane Chasek

I was studying calculus in an abandoned football stadium because it helped me forget the past six months of my life. Studying calculus also felt like something a normal university student would do on an afternoon in mid-March, plus calculus had nothing to do with James Joyce, *Ulysses*, or Irish literature, which were the last things I wanted to think about.

Most people would have felt hopelessly alone sitting in the south wing of Memorial Stadium during the off-season. No players slamming into each other on the gridiron, no raucous fans around me, no music or commentary blaring from the speakers—nothing but silence, a silence made more palpable by the sheer scale of the stadium's emptiness. The windows of the abandoned skyboxes staring down at me vacantly, the empty seats arranged around me like the dark scales of some massive prehistoric fish: this was a place of pure isolation, an isolation that allowed me to withdraw from the world.

I wouldn't be surprised if I was the only person at the University of Nebraska who knew that Memorial Stadium was unlocked and unmonitored this time of year. You could walk through any of the entrances, make your way up the wide, echoing stairs, and pick whichever seat you desired. And if you didn't mind the darkness (the stadium had no power during the off-season) you could make yourself comfortable in one of the skyboxes. Most people, I'm sure, would have been uncomfortable entering an abandoned football stadium in this way, but undiagnosed autism had a way of making me reckless when it came to transgressing social norms. Even as a child, I'd been drawn to unpeopled places—empty fields behind my grandparents' home, abandoned feedlots and factories, the back aisles of grocery stores at 3 a.m. The problems of existing in this world seemed manageable in places like that, where it was just me and my thoughts. Of course, most places are designed with multiple people in mind, which sometimes made life unbearable. But while I struggled to make small talk or form lasting bonds with anyone I met, I was fearless when it came to inhabiting uncannily isolated places like this. And I was going to be expelled soon, so why not break a few more rules?

Bear in mind, I'm not writing this to excuse anything I did during my freshman year of college, and I'm not setting out to make myself seem like a victim. What I did was dishonest, I know that, and I was more than willing to take responsibility for my actions. I wasn't seeking comfort in solitude because I felt wronged; I was seeking this comfort because I realized just how little

I understood the rules of this new world I'd entered. I'd tried to play by the university's social rules, and just when I thought I had them figured out, I'd been struck down before I could savor my success.

High school's social expectations had been so straightforward. But in university, I'd been confronted with an alien set of rules and social codes that weren't quite the rules of childhood and adolescence, nor were they the rules of adulthood. They were somewhere in between. I was quick to notice that no one in college (with the exception of couples) formed "friendships." There were club members, fraternity brothers, sorority sisters, future engineers, future accountants, future grad students, cohorts, colleagues—but no friends. Instead, people formed "connections," which were like friendships, but only on a surface level; in reality, connections were less about connecting with someone on a personal level, and more about getting to know them well enough so that (potentially) they'd remember you and (potentially) do you a favor in the future.

The rules of human conduct had been pulled out from under me. The simple, sincere friendships I'd known in my past life were now nothing more than memories, and I struggled to form even the most superficial human connections. But I soon learned I had something to offer my fellow students—I could "help" them with their English assignments. I wasn't a tutor in the traditional sense (upperclassmen and grad students had that market cornered). Instead, I wrote people's essays for them. I knew it was cheating, but cheating (especially on Fraternity Row) was part and parcel of university life, something a surprising number of students engaged in to get ahead.

The fraternity brothers I worked for also paid handsomely. I did all the assigned reading, outside research, and writing, and they provided me with a small fortune in return. Something I didn't realize about fraternity members when I entered university was that many of them (a majority, actually) come from rich families; so not only did they receive hefty allowances from Mom and Pop for attending class, they also never learned the true value of money. Thus, while your average undergrad from a middle-class family would pay $20-$50 for a five-page essay, your typical fraternity brother would readily pay $200-$300 for that same essay. They never haggled, either. And, sometimes, they felt like friends.

In that first semester, I made almost $10,000. By finals week, I'd earned a reputation as a whiz-kid who, despite only being a freshman, was able to write A-level papers for 300- and 400-level courses. It wasn't hard work, just time-consuming. Without any friends or weekend plans, I had more than enough time to handle my own course load along with the course loads of anyone willing to pay me.

But my career ground to a halt on March 6. That was when I finally got caught.

James Joyce's *Ulysses* was my downfall. The 20-page essay I'd written for the "Cyclops" section was, I believed, some of my most impressive work, especially considering that I'd had to read and annotate the entirety of *Ulysses* in a little under a week, as well as research Irish history and Dublin geography just to make sense of certain chapters. Given that I was a freshman writing a paper for a senior-level course in Irish literature, the fact that I managed to snag a B+ was miraculous. The frat brother I'd written it for felt otherwise. He'd heard I was supposed to deliver A-level work. When he saw that B+ on his paper, he decided to turn me (and, by extension, himself) in to the office of academic affairs.

The University of Nebraska is famous for its football team, and Memorial Stadium, during Husker home games, is one of the most densely-populated spots in the entire Midwest. But now, I had the stadium all to myself. I'd started my university career alone, and now I was ending it alone, uselessly studying for a class I wasn't going to complete. After my meeting with the Dean of Arts and Sciences, which was scheduled for tomorrow, I'd be gone.

Isolation has always possessed a clarity that I've never been able to find in human company. The noises of new settings, new social rules and customs, the constant race to win friends and influence people—I'd grown tired of it all. To a certain extent, I'd grown tired of literature as well. Especially James Joyce. Derivatives, integrals, rotating functions around axes, finding the volumes and surface areas of irregular solids—it was elegant, complex, time-consuming. Just like my new life. But unlike my new life, calculus was built on axioms, inviolable rules that didn't change from one setting to the next. For all its challenges, calculus made sense and never stopped making sense once you finally learned it.

Newton and Leibniz had each independently developed calculus, solitary thinkers who, distancing themselves from civilization, had changed mathematics forever. Ever since I was a kid, I'd fantasized about a similar isolation. In this fantasy, I'm the last human on Earth. The events leading up to my isolation were always unimportant, though I preferred a scenario in which the rest of my fellow humans leave Earth to settle Mars or some nearby star system. What mattered, ultimately, was the solitude itself, the vacancy of all Earth's major cities and buildings—everything empty and silent for me to enjoy.

In that silence, I felt (or imagined I felt) a low, throbbing hum beneath my seat. There was a legend I'd heard when I first came to the University of Nebraska, the legend of the supercomputer Deep Red (a portmanteau of Big Red, the moniker for our football team, and the famous chess-playing computer Deep Blue), which was allegedly housed beneath Memorial Stadium. In all likelihood, Deep Red didn't exist, but if I focused hard enough, ignored the birdsong of spring, I could almost hear the whirring of its circuits deep beneath the earth.

This chapter of my life was fast coming to a close. I couldn't imagine what would happen in the days or months to come, but I had a feeling life was only going to get harder, more incomprehensible.

I turned to an empty page in my notebook, began a new story for myself to inhabit. If I couldn't make it in this world, I could create my own world:

I'm the last human today. I was the last human yesterday. I will be the last human tomorrow.

I've found a comfortable stadium in which to spend the rest of my days. I've started studying calculus, something I'd meant to do when I had other humans to keep me company. Now, I have nothing to occupy my mind but the ideas of Newton and Leibniz. I like to think that, in my small way, I'm preserving their memories.

There's a ceaseless hum beneath my feet. It courses through the concrete of the stadium, rhythmic and soothing, as if I'm living above the burrow of some massive subterranean beast. I wonder what lies beneath me.

In the Last Days of the Kingdom

Maria Bolaños

The plane idles on the tarmac, heavy and bloated as a beached whale
    The subway is a hollow snakeskin
The unfinished freeway undoes itself, decaying
    wood beams exposed like bones jutting from carcass.

On the street the people walk quickly, dark heads bowed, faces covered.
    They say nothing to one another, make no eye contact, knowing
        each stare can become steel, a knife to the face.

A nurse collapses in the break room.
    Death makes rounds through the hallways, knocking softly on doors
        of the old ones waiting for a visit.

The rich gather inside a mansion of marble and alabaster
    They sip on crystal champagne glasses full of bleach
        to become white on the inside, too.

They bury the nurse.

Semi-trucks are parked
on the side of the road. Inside their trailers, bodies
heaped and rotting: the cemeteries are full.

The car groans into the driveway like an old dog searching for someplace to die.

And she talks to herself in an empty room
and his hair grows long and his body curves to the shape of the table

and their noses sting from the alcohol
and their palms turn slick
and their knuckles raw

               from washing
                    their clothes by hand
               from washing
                    off the careless coughs of others
               from washing
                    the day from every last cell of skin

Over the shuffle of papers, of sound
    mind and body, they listen
        for the phone to give news.

                        The ones behind glass
                        wish for home.

Each minute is a question: *Am I ready to head this house?*
                                Am I ready to support all the families back home?
                                Am I ready to die?

A skyline cuts uneven teeth
                    an animal's mouth in one long and pleading gasp

invocation of the mother
Rachel Randolph

why has it taken 20 years to
teach me that God is not a father

when I picture that
white skinned gray beard
Santa Claus type of God
I do not feel any sort of
kinship but

when I imagine the mother
when I sit on sunset grass warm
and wet beneath my toes

I can feel her welcoming me home

Brief Encounters at 4AM

Dominic Hemy

You need at least half a dozen hidey holes, little refuges to cycle through in case anyone else got to one first, or too many people are passing by on certain nights. Occasionally you stumble across a right gem – a small block of flats with a rarely locked front door, for example. No noise, residual heat seeping out into the communal areas, sometimes even a clean carpeted floor. It does mean staying out longer to ensure the residents are safely tucked up in bed, but particularly earlier in the week, these are the jackpot. Although you do need to keep them to yourself, camaraderie only stretches so far.

Something's trapped under the door, a bag or a newspaper probably. Oof, this is really wedged in. I know I'm tired, but it's not that heavy. Alright, big push. *Crack*. That didn't sound good.

"Ow!"

"Shit!"

Who? What? Why? Get in get in get in. I hope I didn't hurt him.

"Are you okay?"

"Er, yeah..."

I can't open the lock fast enough. Must get in. Why is there someone asleep in front of my door? Fuck, dropped my keys. Help. Why me? C'mon, here we go. In, click, bolt. Fuck.

"Tess! Tess! There's a man outside our door!"

"Huh? Wa...?" Sleep clogs her eyes, and confusion reigns.

"Outside, man, why?"

"What do you mean, Mags?"

"Peep hole, look – there's a man asleep against the stairwell door."

We take turns to look, leaving rings of perspiration on the wood. He seems dazed, but wanders out of sight. The light upstairs turns on, and I hear a door bang shut. He's not leaving. Now what?

Thump. Thump. Thump. *Crack*. Christ that hurts! Right on the crown too. The automatic light pings into life, and my head swims horribly. Still dark out, so who the fuck is trying to come through now? As I roll over, she forces her way in.

"Are you okay?"

"Er, yeah…"

Can't quite focus, everything is a bit black and white. She drops her keys, the metallic jangle piercing right through my skull. Running inside, I hear locks and bolts click into place before being able to focus. What time does she call this? Seriously though, what time is it? There are muffled voices behind that door, but everywhere else seems silent. I'd best move, just in case: upstairs should be fine, doubt the ruckus disturbed them. And I was having such a nice dream, too…

Alex has texted me, worried that he seems to be home before me. How do I explain this? Sod it, I'll just call him. It sounds even more ridiculous as I recount it all.

"Tess has got next door's number and is messaging her to see if she knows him. I've found the non-emergency police number."

"Nonono, call 999. There's a strange man wandering around your flats at 4am, I think this counts as an emergency."

"Possibly. Maybe he's just homeless."

"Yes, probably. But it's the two of you there and at least one woman next door. I don't even want to think of what else it could be."

"Okay, you're right. Tess, Alex thinks we should ring 999." She nods. "I'm going to hang up so I can. I'll call you back once I've spoken to them."

I can't get comfortable again. Stupid bitch, that spot was bloody perfect. Let's try on the ground floor, I think I saw a spot out of the way down there. Nope, far too drafty. That breeze under the door is something wicked. And the bike definitely has a sinister look to it. Back upstairs I go. Not sure I'm going to get back to sleep again at this rate.

Tossing and turning, but I think I've lost this fight. Oh don't tell me that was the front door. More people? I cannot catch a break tonight. Sounds like a few of them. Bollocking bollocksy bollocks, the police.

"Oh, good evening Pat, fancy finding you hiding here."

And of course it is officer 7429, so I won't even get a nice cell for a couple hours undisturbed shut-eye to finish the night.

"Just trying to keep off the streets, like you asked me."

"With a little side-line in scaring young women?"

"Look, how was I supposed to know she would be coming back so late?"

"Hope you're not paying too much rent for these digs."

"Fuck off."

"Now, now, Pat, no need for that."

"So are you going to take me back to the station, or what?"

"I don't think so, it's almost dawn — can't you hear the birds warming up? Time for you to be on your way. C'mon then, let's escort you to the high street."

Fuck my life.

Fuck my life, will nothing go right? Can't I have just one evening without everything going wrong, please? The upstairs freezer, line cleaning taking forever, whiny Art being so rude, and now this random... It is only Monday. I can hear the murmuring of voices out there, and the lights keep going on and off, but I am too scared to check. What is the cat up to?

"Have you given Trix catnip? It's like she's on speed and acid at the same time. She's fallen off the sofa for the fourth time, and is being surprised by her own back paws every ten seconds." I'm going to video call Alex, he'll love this display.

"No, of course not. Well, I don't think so... Let me see if I can find the packaging for her new toy. I'll be pissed off if it does have any."

"Good luck trying to get it off her if it does."

The distraction is a relief, however brief. I can still hear movement outside. The chances of sleep now are rapidly approaching zero. And I'm meeting up with Heather tomorrow, what a barrel of laughs that will be. Fuck my life.

the past is a jean jacket
Cloud Delfina

when I open my mouth   another
                                                        person comes out
            she changes her outfit
                        depending on who
                                    she's talking to

she wears her gold hoops
            and red lipstick
on most days
            she struggles to be
                                    bare-faced
even when I talk to her

do you ever forget
                        who you are
                                    until someone else says your name?

                                    sometimes
                                    I'm so lonely
                                                I practice
                                                            casual conversations
                                                                        in my car

sometimes I talk to myself
                        all serious
                                    updating me
                                                about my latest tragedy

most times
it makes me laugh

I can be so dramatic

my bad habit is
looking through
old photos
I make visits
to all my past selves

my oversized jean jacket
and velvet ballet flat
pins that announce
my coolness
trying to be
whatever it was
I thought
the room wanted me to be

at night I close my eyes
and walk into rooms
I find myself at the pool table
losing horribly to You

You are singing a James Brown song
on the touchtunes jukebox
The song I picked
is twenty minutes out

It plays long after I leave

I don't notice that I left
        I spend the night looking for myself
                in the backseat
                    in the street
                        in the backyard
                        of our friend's house

I am nowhere to be found.

Contributor Bios

Los Angeles-born **Rachel Alarcio**'s work has appeared in or is forthcoming in two award-winning WriteGirl anthologies, *Primeval Monster*, *Zero Readers*, *Lines & Breaks*, *The Bitchin' Kitsch*, *Red Ogre Review*, *You Might Need To Hear This*, *Exposition Review*, at LAX's Terminal 7-8, and elsewhere. They are a Scholastic Art & Writing Awards Silver Medalist in Short Story. She is currently working towards her B.A. in English from Kalamazoo College. Find them @rachelalarcio on Twitter, @raechillout on Instagram, and rachelalarcio.com.

Ash Bainbridge is a queer student midwife and poet mentored by The Word Association. They spotlight identities in the shadows and exposes binaries for what they are. Publications include "Scottish BloodPlay" (*Bleeding Thunder*, 2021) and "Mumpa" (*Songs of Love and Strength*, 2021). On 29 June 2022, Ash performed "Simone Says…" to mark Pride as a protest for #NotSafeToBeMe. Their performance of "My Best Estimate" (2022) was described by Jonny Fluffypunk as, "Bloody hell, spot on."

Eleanor Ball is a writer from Des Moines, Iowa. She studies Public Health and English at The George Washington University, where she's currently conducting research on The Lais of Marie de France. Her work is featured / forthcoming in Stone of Madness, Bullshit Lit, and The B'K.

Camden Beal is a current undergraduate at Arizona State University, where he studies English Literature. In his free time, he enjoys writing, reading, cooking, and spending time with loved ones and friends. His work carries a strong focus on personal identity, grief, loss, and impermanence.

Maria Bolaños (she/they) is a Filipina American poet and co-Founder of Sampaguita Press. She is committed to building spaces to nurture and showcase Filipinxao literature as well as Black, Indigenous, and POC literature. Her poems were nominated for Best of the Net in 2021 and 2022, and her writing has been featured in publications such as Touchstone, Cut Fruit Collective's Cut Fruit Stories, and decomp journal, among others. She is the author of the poetry chapbook, SANA (Sampaguita Press, 2022). See more of their work on Instagram @mariabeewrites.

Cloud Delfina Cardona (she/they) is a poet born and raised in San Antonio, Texas. She is the author of *What Remains*, winner of the 2020 Host Publications Chapbook Award. Her poems have appeared in *Apogee Journal*, *Cosmonauts Avenue*, *Salt Hill Journal*, and many more. In Fall 2019, she co-founded *Infrarrealista Review*, a literary journal for Texan writers, with Linda Rivas Vázquez. She currently teaches high school English on the south side of San Antonio.

Monica Colón is a Salvadoran/American writer from Waco, Texas. She has lived and studied in the Chicago suburbs and Querétaro, Mexico. Her poems have been featured in *Susurrus Magazine*, *Cool Rock Repository*, and Paddler Press. She is a Pushcart Prize nominee and the winner of the 2021 Iris N. Spencer Sonnet Contest from West Chester University Poetry Center.

Lane Chasek is the author of a nonfiction novel, a novel, a collection of poems, and two chapbooks. Lane's work has appeared in *Hobart*, *perhappened*, *North Dakota Quarterly*, and many other publications.

Anna Everts is a non-binary autistic writer and artist from the Netherlands. They mainly write comics, but also dabble in creating collages and occasionally in painting. Their work is mostly inspired by the things they see around them, with hints of their own history here and there. When they're not writing or crafting, they like to watch series, read and take photos of things that catch their eye.

Ash/ley Frenkel (they/she) is an artist of dabbling and educator born and living in Brooklyn, NY. They like to doodle and paint, read, kiss, play in the kitchen, observe, and laugh, all of which informs their sometimes dramatic, often yearning, and usually existential poetry. They were recently published in *Relevant Poetry*, a collection released by Irrelevant Press.

Max Gillette is an English major at Central Michigan University, where they work as an editor for two student-led publications: *The Honors Platform* and *Great Lakes Platform*. Their poetry has appeared in or is forthcoming from *Spoonie Press*, *Cutbow Quarterly*, *Morning Fruit*, *Red Cedar Review*, and other publications.

Noll Griffin is a California-raised illustrator and printmaker of the linoleum carving variety currently based in Berlin, Germany. When not working on art, he enjoys fermenting food and playing Berlin's acoustic open mic scene.

Julian Guy is a trans and queer writer born in Reno, NV. Their work can be found in *The Adroit Journal*, *Lesbians are Miracles*, *Wrongdoing Magazine*, and more. In their free time find them in the garden, with their feet in the river, or covered in sand at the beach. They are online at julianguy.com.

Denis Harnedy is a barrister living and working in Dublin. He has recently begun writing poetry with two distinct sources of inspiration – his year of living in Lucan (a suburb of Dublin) from November 2020 to November 2021 (much of it during lockdown) and his reading of Chinese history. He has previously been published in *Impossible Archetype* and in *Shearsman Magazine*.

Dominic Hemy is a Londoner tired of London, and generally exhausted by everything else. He did once grow up (a mistake he vows never to make again), whilst now hoping to spend the rest of his days creatively pottering. Complete with beer in hand, obviously.

Sagaree Jain (they/them) is a poet, writer, artist, and queer. Their writing has been featured in *Autostraddle*, *The Margins*, *them. magazine*, and *The Offing*, where they are also an Assistant Editor. Their collaborative poetry collection with Arati Warrier, *Longing and Other Heirlooms*, is the winner of the Eggtooth Editions Chapbook Contest and is out now, and their book *SHRINES* will be out from Game Over Books in 2023. They tweet at @sagareej.

Robin Kinzer is a queer, disabled poet and sometimes memoirist. She was once a communist beaver in a PBS documentary. She is now an MFA candidate at University of Baltimore. Robin has poems recently published, or shortly forthcoming in *Little Patuxent Review*, fifth wheel press, *Corporeal Lit*, *Defunkt Magazine*, and others. She loves glitter, Ferris wheels, waterfalls, and radical kindness. She can be found on Twitter at @RobinAKinzer.

Arah Ko is a writer from Hawai'i. Her work has appeared in *Sidereal*, *Fugue*, *Sugar House Review*, *The Margins*, *Hyphen*, and elsewhere. She is the Art Editor for *The Journal*. Catch her at arahko.com.

Madeline Langan is an artist, writer, and architecture student pursuing her Bachelor of Architecture from Pratt Institute with a minor in Literature and Writing. Her work has appeared in *The Prattler*, *Scud*, and Ursus Americanus Press's *Landfill*. She can also be found modeling tiny houses, rereading *Wuthering Heights*, and watering her plants. Web: madelinelangan.cargo.site

Kit Lascher is the King of Trash Wonderland. Her theatrical pieces have been produced across the US. Favorite artistic projects include creating "Recover: A Cabaret by and for People with Mental Illness," publishing zines with *WolfShark Press*, and writing and directing for Reboot Theatre Company and Copious Love. You can find her work in *beestung*, in upcoming collaborations as part of her residency with Nomadic Soundsters, and in more spaces to be announced.

Suzanne Lavallee (She/Her) is a writer based in a small town in New England. She is a college student studying Professional and Creative Writing. Suzanne has been writing since the age of fourteen and looks to pursue a career as a published author.

Jennifer Martelli is the author of *The Queen of Queens* and *My Tarantella*, named a "Must Read" by the Massachusetts Center for the Book. Her work has appeared in *Poetry*, *The Academy of American Poets Poem-a-Day*, *The Indianapolis Review*, and elsewhere. Jennifer Martelli has twice received grants for poetry from the Massachusetts Cultural Council. She is co-poetry editor for *Mom Egg Review*.

Colleen McDermott (she/they) hails from southeast Pennsylvania and currently studies at Washington University in St. Louis. Equal parts aspiring author and aspiring wildland firefighter, they aim to explore themes of placemaking, identity, and nature. Their writing has appeared in many documents on their computer, with the hope to someday add some publication titles to this sentence.

SIMONE PARKER is a queer midwestern Jew, plant enthusiast, collage artist and poet. Her writing has appeared in *Tusitala Literary Magazine* and the independently published *Poets Igniting Change Zine*, and she has been a featured poet at The Poetry Foundation's The Open Door Readings in Chicago. She lives in Minneapolis with two cats named after beer and a husband named after the coolest kid in his mom's fifth grade class. Find her on Instagram @singedfingers.

Amie Pascal is a lesbian artist and writer whose work is in continual conversation with the paths from life to death, from seasonal flowers to chronic illness, and the stories we tell along the way about ourselves and each other. Amie uses her queer feminist lens to make sense of self, community, and time through her art.

Nathan Pettigrew was born and raised an hour south of New Orleans and lives in the Tampa area with his loving wife. His stories have appeared in *Deep South Magazine*, *Penumbra Online*, *"The Year" Anthology* from Crack the Spine, *Stoneboat*, *Cowboy Jamboree*, and the *Nasty: Fetish Fights Back* anthology from Anna Yeatts of *Flash Fiction Online*, which was spotlighted in a 2017 *Rolling Stone* article.

Rachel Randolph (she/her) is an undergraduate writing major at Lipscomb University. She was born and raised on a small farm just outside of Nashville, TN. She loves to write across many genres, including short stories, poetry, and braided essays. Her work explores the divinity of being human and the magic that we take for granted in our daily lives.

nat raum (b. 1996) is a disabled artist, writer, and genderless disaster based on occupied Piscataway land in Baltimore, MD. They're a current MFA candidate and also the editor-in-chief of fifth wheel press. Past and upcoming publishers of their writing include *Delicate Friend*, *perhappened*, *CLOVES*, and *trampset*. Find them online: natraum.com/links.

Ruthenium (they/them) is an artist currently living in the state of uncertainty. They believe creativity is real-life magic, and are obsessed with texture, context, light, and the question "what if?..." Their art has been published in Rabble Review, Celestite Poetry, Vulnerary Magazine, Messy Misfits Magazine, and Warning Lines Literary, among other wonderful places. Their various presences and publications can be found at https://linktr.ee/Ruthenium

Syd Shaw is a poet from the San Fernando Valley. She writes about love, witchcraft, and body horror. Syd is Assistant Poetry Editor at *Passengers Journal*, and has a degree in creative writing from Northwestern University. She has previously been published in *Cathexis Northwest*, *Ember Chasm*, *Waxing & Waning*, *Eclectica Magazine*, *Panoply Zine*, and *The London Reader*, among others. Her passions include tarot, guitar, and aerial silks. Syd's work can be found at sydshaw.carrd.co

Kate Suddes is trying to break your heart. Her writing has appeared in *A Cup of Jo, Romper, HuffPost, NAILED Magazine, Ravishly, Noteworthy, Human Parts & The Manifest-Station.* She is currently at work on her first book about her stillborn son, Paul.

Dilinna Ugochukwu is a Nigerian American writer from Southern California. Their work is published or forthcoming in *Rigorous Magazine*, the *Blue Marble Review*, and *Tab Journal*.

Christopher Wellings is a queer poet based in Brighton, UK, with an academic background in sexual dissidence and cultural change. His poetry has appeared in *Queerlings* magazine and been long listed for the UK's 2021 National Poetry Competition. He is currently working on poetry exploring the intersections of queerness, religion and OCD.

Nico Wilkinson is a poet, organizer and artist based out of Colorado Springs, CO. From 2017-2022, they founded and facilitated the Quaill Club, an intentional living community for queer artists and farmers. They are the organizer of "Keep Colorado Springs Queer," an award-winning open mic by and for the queer community of Colorado Springs. They are always trying their best.

Taylor Yingshi is a sophomore at Columbia University making finely detailed, undulating illustrations inspired by a confluence of aesthetics — from the exuberance of Baroque paintings to the granularity of modern digital art. Her work revolves around the preservation and transformation of memory, history, and heritage. Find her on Twitter and Instagram @yingshiart, or at tayloryingshi.com.